Mastering Retail Security

A Guide for Loss Prevention and Store Management Excellence

By

Antonio Rosa

Acknowledgments

Special thanks to João Coutinho for all
help with this book

Note

Basic training program for shopkeepers, watchers and others linked to the retail industry, retail, and large commercial areas.

This training program serves to complement the basic needs of combating organized and non-organized crime in commercial establishments.

Índice

In the intricate dance between supply and demand, big stores have emerged as colossal players significantly shaping economies across the globe. These sprawling retail spaces, adorned with an extensive array of products, stand as iconic symbols of consumer culture, shaping economic landscapes worldwide.

Tracing the roots of big stores takes us back to the late 19th century, marked by the birth of department stores that revolutionized retail by centralizing a diverse array of goods. The mid-20th century witnessed the rise of hypermarkets, seamlessly integrating supermarkets and department stores under one roof, propelling big stores into expansive hubs catering to diverse consumer needs. Big stores, often synonymous with retail giants, transcend their physical dimensions to wield significant economic influence.

Their colossal operations generate employment, stimulate manufacturing sectors, and contribute substantially to tax revenues. The ripple effect of their expansive supply chains resonates across industries such as logistics, packaging, and marketing.

The proliferation of big stores aligns seamlessly with the rise of consumerism, a driving force in the contemporary retail landscape. Consumers, enticed by the convenience and variety offered by big stores, play a pivotal role in propelling the sector's growth. The ever-evolving dynamics of retail, influenced by urbanization, shifting demographics, and technological innovations, continue to mold the strategies of these retail behemoths.

In the 21st century, big stores stand at the forefront of technological integration, transforming the shopping experience into a digital marvel. Smart shelving, automated inventory management systems, and artificial intelligence-driven customer service redefine the retail landscape, enhancing operational efficiency and providing invaluable data insights into consumer behavior.

The advent of data analytics has emerged as a game-changer in the retail sector, with big stores harnessing information to decode consumer preferences.

Analyzing purchasing patterns, demographics, and market trends allows these establishments to optimize product assortments, pricing strategies, and promotional campaigns, fostering a more personalized and engaging shopping experience.

Big stores navigate the complex global economic landscape, facing challenges such as economic downturns, geopolitical uncertainties, and global pandemics. The resilience of these establishments is tested as they adapt through strategies like diversified offerings and digital transformation to mitigate the impact of external uncertainties.

Sustainability takes center stage in the retail narrative, with big stores leading the charge in adopting eco-friendly practices and ethical standards. From reducing plastic usage to incorporating sustainable sourcing, these establishments are actively addressing their environmental impact, aligning with the growing consumer demand for responsible business practices.

The rise of e-commerce poses a formidable challenge to traditional brick-and-mortar stores, including big stores. Embracing digital channels and crafting omnichannel strategies become imperative to meet evolving consumer expectations and maintain relevance in the changing retail landscape.

As nations strive for economic recovery, big stores emerge as crucial catalysts, stimulating consumer spending, creating employment opportunities, and contributing to the broader economic ecosystem. Governments recognize the significance of the retail sector, often implementing policies to support its growth post-crisis.

The future trajectory of big stores remains speculative, influenced by emerging trends, technological advancements, and evolving consumer expectations. Potential avenues for growth include the integration of augmented reality, further personalization through data analytics, and the seamless convergence of online and offline experiences. Sustainability initiatives are poised to intensify, with big stores becoming standard-bearers for environmentally conscious retail practices.

In summation, big stores transcend their role as mere retail spaces; they embody the pulse of consumer culture and economic vitality.

Their evolutionary journey mirrors societal shifts, technological progress, and the relentless pursuit of meeting consumer needs.

As big stores continue to adapt, innovate, and contribute to the global economy, their role remains central to the ever-evolving narrative of retail.

In the dynamic realm of retail and big stores, security emerges as a linchpin, playing a multifaceted role that extends beyond mere surveillance. It encompasses a broader spectrum of functions, from protecting diverse assets to mitigating losses and ensuring the trust of both customers and employees. In this commercial landscape, safeguarding assets goes beyond the merchandise on the shelves.

Big stores house an array of valuable resources, including physical infrastructure and intellectual property, making them susceptible to various threats. The scope of security measures is extensive, aiming to protect against theft, fraud, and operational discrepancies that can profoundly impact the economic viability of these establishments.

Loss prevention becomes a cornerstone of security, demanding a proactive stance to anticipate potential threats and mitigate risks. The economic toll of theft and fraud is significant, affecting profit margins and, in some cases, the very survival of retail businesses.

Security investments, therefore, translate into economic prudence, safeguarding the bottom line and contributing to the overall sustainability of big stores.

The delicate construct of customer trust in the retail space relies heavily on security measures. Customers need assurance that their shopping experience is safe and secure. Visible security measures, from surveillance cameras to uniformed personnel, play a pivotal role in instilling confidence and fostering the perception of the store as a haven for consumers.

Internal accountability is a crucial facet of security, extending beyond external threats to encompass employee theft, fraud, and negligence. Implementing security measures fosters a culture of accountability among employees, emphasizing the shared responsibility of safeguarding the store's assets. Technological innovations have transformed the security dynamics in retail.

Cutting-edge technologies such as artificial intelligence, data analytics, and facial recognition not only enhance surveillance capabilities but also provide valuable insights into customer behavior. These innovations optimize store layouts and product placements for both security and commercial objectives.

Security measures prove their relevance in unforeseen challenges, ranging from natural disasters to public emergencies. Robust crisis management protocols, including evacuation plans and emergency response systems, ensure the safety of both customers and employees during unforeseen crises.

Regulatory compliance is a critical aspect of security in retail, with the sector subject to various regulations and standards. Adhering to these legal frameworks is a testament to the commitment of big stores to ethical and responsible business practices.

In the digital age, cybersecurity becomes an integral part of security measures. Big stores, with their online platforms and extensive use of data, are vulnerable to cyber threats. Cybersecurity measures, including encryption and robust data protection protocols, are essential for preserving the integrity of customer information.

The perceived safety quotient significantly influences the public image of big stores. A retail establishment known for its commitment to security not only attracts more customers but also cultivates a positive reputation in the market.

In conclusion, security in retail and big stores transcends the role of a discretionary expense, emerging as an imperative investment. Its impacts encompass financial stability, customer trust, employee accountability, and the overall resilience of these commercial giants.

As big stores navigate the complexities of an ever-evolving retail landscape, security measures stand as stalwart guardians, ensuring a safe and prosperous shopping environment for all stakeholders.

Introducing the culture of safety in companies

In the contemporary landscape marked by diverse threats, the nexus between criminal activities and personal methods has intensified, presenting an intricate web of challenges. Crime, once tangible and overt, has evolved into a nearly imperceptible entity, further exacerbated by the complexities arising from the ongoing COVID-19 pandemic. As the number and nature of threats have multiplied, so have the vulnerabilities across various domains.

Organizations, spanning business enterprises, service centers, shopping facilities, and beyond, find themselves compelled to navigate this intricate landscape of risks to accomplish their objectives. While security has traditionally stood as a conspicuous pillar of growth, its positioning within the broader administrative structures has often been peripheral.

However, risk management extends beyond mere physical security concerns; it encompasses financial, reputational, and legal dimensions, emphasizing the critical role security should play at these pivotal junctures within companies.

The symbiotic relationship between risk and security transcends mere linguistic nuances; it necessitates a systematic approach for effective integration. A paradigm shift is imperative, wherein security ceases to be an isolated department and, instead, becomes an integral part of the organizational fabric. This metamorphosis is essential for security to not only enhance the protective measures but also to serve as a strategic force, influencing management decisions across the corporate spectrum.

To foster an effective security culture within your organization, several key considerations must be addressed, expanding upon the fundamental aspects outlined in your initial text. Let's delve into the broader realm of security culture, elucidating its significance and providing actionable insights to cultivate a robust security ethos within your company.

Understanding Security Culture

Holistic Approach to Risk Management:

Inculcating a security culture begins with adopting a holistic approach to risk management. This involves not only safeguarding physical assets but also addressing financial, reputational, and legal risks. A comprehensive risk assessment should be conducted to identify and mitigate potential threats across all dimensions.

Business Continuity Planning:

A crucial aspect of effective risk management is ensuring business continuity. Establishing and maintaining a robust security framework becomes imperative to mitigate disruptions. This involves devising contingency plans, regularly testing them, and incorporating lessons learned to enhance overall resilience.

Integration of Physical and Logical Security:

The integration of physical and logical security measures is paramount in today's interconnected landscape. This convergence ensures a unified and comprehensive defense against a spectrum of threats, ranging from cyberattacks to physical intrusions. Implementing technologies that bridge these domains fosters a more resilient security posture.

Corporate Security Structure and Communication Channels:

To embed security into the organizational DNA, a well-defined corporate security structure should be established. This structure should delineate roles, responsibilities, and reporting lines. Clear communication channels must be instituted to facilitate the flow of information, ensuring swift responses to emerging threats.

Security Training and Awareness Programs:

A robust security culture thrives on the awareness and proactive participation of every individual within the organization. Implementing regular security training programs, both for physical and cyber threats, empowers employees to be vigilant and responsive. This human-centric approach is pivotal in fortifying the organization's overall security posture.

Continuous Monitoring and Adaptation:

Security is a dynamic field, and threats evolve over time. Establishing mechanisms for continuous monitoring, threat intelligence integration, and adaptive security practices is imperative. Regularly reassessing the security landscape allows organizations to stay ahead of emerging risks.

Legal and Regulatory Compliance:

A robust security culture extends beyond internal policies; it encompasses adherence to legal and regulatory frameworks. Ensuring compliance not only mitigates legal risks but also enhances the organization's reputation as a responsible and trustworthy entity.

The Evolution of Security within Organizations

The metamorphosis of security within organizations is not merely a structural realignment; it is a cultural shift that permeates every facet of the corporate environment.

By assimilating security into the organizational DNA, ompanies can proactively navigate the complexities of the modern threat landscape, positioning themselves as resilient entities capable of safeguarding their interests and those of their stakeholders.

The integration of security into the organizational culture is a strategic imperative for modern enterprises.

This shift from a compartmentalized security approach to a pervasive security culture is not only a response to the evolving threat landscape but a proactive stance that positions organizations to thrive amidst uncertainty. Embracing this evolution requires commitment, investment, and a shared understanding that security is not a department; it is a mindset that permeates every level of the organizational hierarchy.

Integration

The seamless integration of Corporate Security is paramount, necessitating its adaptation into all facets of business management processes within companies. The incorporation of security measures should be pervasive, extending across the entire organizational framework.

Earnings

Corporate security aligns with business-focused criteria, framed within the context of costs and investments. Centralized management emerges as a strategic approach, facilitating an overarching reduction in costs and enhancing the overall efficacy of applied security efforts.

Business Continuity

The presence of the security department is imperative throughout all decision cycles within the business structure to ensure comprehensive business continuity. A well-defined safety cycle encompasses protection, prevention, detection, response, and recovery, underscoring the holistic nature of security considerations.

Adjustable

Flexibility is a cornerstone for the security department, necessitating adaptation to influential top-level decisions. A nuanced understanding of financial impacts, as well as the ramifications of security measures on business continuity and customer relationships, is crucial. Each security project should undergo a corporate risk analysis phase to discern its advantages and disadvantages. Notably, security directors should extend their risk studies beyond physical aspects, encompassing the broader impact of measures and investments on projects.

Relationships and Knowledge

Establishing a symbiotic relationship between administrations and security is pivotal for informed decision-making. It is imperative for those responsible for security to possess a nuanced understanding of business management, ensuring the viability of all projects.

This interplay between security and business acumen is instrumental in navigating the intricate landscape where security imperatives align with the strategic goals of the organization.

Introduction

The ramifications of inventory loss, stemming from theft, inadequate control, or other factors, extend beyond the immediate financial hit. The inability to recover the costs of lost goods directly impacts a company's bottom line, as there is nothing available for sale or return. Some companies, to offset the costs associated with stock shortages, may resort to increasing prices for customers.

However, this represents an ineffective risk transfer strategy, burdening customers due to management inefficiencies.

Such a strategy can prove detrimental, especially considering that certain customers are price sensitive. Consequently, losses not only affect the financial standing of the company but can also strain customer relationships and impede sales growth.

The primary objective of implementing loss control measures is two-fold:

Increase Sales for Improved Profitability:
By mitigating losses and ensuring a robust inventory management system, companies can enhance sales, directly contributing to improved overall profitability.

Control Losses through Inventory Management:
Efficient control mechanisms are essential for optimizing inventory results, preventing losses, and safeguarding the financial health of the organization.

Understanding the multifaceted nature of inventory reduction, it's crucial to delve into the various types of theft that contribute to these losses. There are three primary categories:

Internal Theft:

Occurs when employees engage in activities leading to inventory shrinkage, jeopardizing the internal integrity of the organization.

External Theft:

Involves theft perpetrated by individuals outside the organization, such as shoplifting, contributing to inventory losses.

External with Internal Involvement:

A hybrid category where external entities collude with internal staff, exacerbating the challenges of inventory control.

Types of inventory reduction in greater detail

Shoplifting or Shrinkage:

Unlawful appropriation of goods by external entities within the retail space.

Fraud in Returns:

Dishonest practices related to product returns, leading to financial losses for the retailer.

Employee Thefts:

Illicit activities by internal staff, including pilferage or misappropriation of inventory.

Administrative Errors:

Mistakes in record-keeping, documentation, or procedural oversights that result in inventory discrepancies.

Supplier Fraud:

Deceptive practices by suppliers that compromise the integrity of the supply chain and contribute to inventory losses.

Unattributed Loss:

Inventory shrinkage that cannot be directly linked to specific causes, posing a challenge for effective prevention.

By comprehensively understanding the nuances of loss prevention and the varied sources of inventory reduction, businesses can tailor their strategies to fortify their defenses, minimize losses, and foster sustained growth in a competitive market.

Safety culture

In the realm of the direct trading industry, fostering a robust safety culture has become imperative. The escalating incidents within home appliance stores, supermarkets, and various establishments dealing in essential items underscore the need for a proactive approach to instigate a paradigm shift in how safety is perceived within our establishments.

The cultivation and promotion of an effective and pragmatic safety culture stand as fundamental pillars for any institution, organization, or infrastructure. This culture serves as a potent mitigator against a spectrum of threats capable of inflicting physical, reputational, financial, and organizational harm.

A genuine safety culture crystallizes through a collective adherence to shared values, permeating every level of the organization. It represents a concerted effort to instill a pervasive sense of security and advocate for practices that are universally embraced.

This, in turn, contributes to the development of a safety-aware workforce, fostering the desired safety behaviors among all occupants of a given space, workplace, or educational institution.

The advantages inherent in cultivating an effective safety culture are manifold:

Engaged Workforce: A workforce that is more likely to actively engage with and take ownership of security issues within the organization.

Enhanced Compliance: Increased adherence to security protection measures, ensuring a more secure environment for all stakeholders.

Risk Mitigation: Reduced risk of incidents involving students, teachers, and employees, thereby safeguarding the well-being of all individuals.

Security Threat Awareness: Heightened awareness of the most pertinent security threats, enabling proactive measures to address potential challenges.

Promotion of Safety-Conscious Behavior: Individuals, including students, teachers, and employees, are more inclined to think and act in a safety-conscious manner.

Increased Sensitivity to Security: A general elevation in sensitivity to the importance of security as a pervasive theme throughout the organization.

Organizations are urged to integrate and uphold an effective security culture where the responsibility for security is a collective endeavor shared by everyone within the organizational ecosystem.

By fostering a culture that prioritizes safety, entities can fortify their defenses, cultivate a vigilant and responsible workforce, and ultimately create environments that are secure, resilient, and conducive to the well-being of all.

Typologies of crimes associated with losses:

Fraud:

Returns Fraud

Among the often-overlooked contributors to retail losses, returns fraud stands out as a significant concern. This form of illicit activity tends to fly under the radar, given that it occurs under certain pressures and can be challenging to detect initially. Its impact becomes apparent over time as losses accumulate throughout the year.

- Returns fraud manifests in various ways, including:
- Return of stolen goods
- Return of goods acquired with counterfeit currency.
- Return of used goods.
- Utilization of manipulated receipts to return merchandise.

Exchanged Goods Returns

The challenge of managing returns is particularly pronounced compared to in-store shoplifting due to the myriad ways in which it can occur. Nevertheless, combating fraud in returns is possible with a well-crafted return-and-exchange policy consistently applied by vigilant employees. Key strategies include:

Receipt Requirement for Cash Returns: Most retailers mandate a receipt for cash refunds on returned items, and it is advisable to adopt a similar policy. Without a receipt, customers should be ineligible for a cash refund, limiting the recourse to store credit or item exchange. The implementation of this policy should align with the store's trade and return guidelines.

Employee Training on Fraud Detection: Unlike thefts, fraudulent returns are not as overt. Therefore, training employees to identify and thwart fraud in returns becomes imperative. Equipping staff with the skills to discern subtle signs of fraudulent activities is crucial for the effective prevention of losses.

Request an ID to track returns

Request for ID Verification for Return Tracking:

To enhance the effectiveness of your return and staff training policies, consider implementing a mandatory ID verification process during all return and exchange transactions. This measure serves to identify and flag customers engaged in frequent or suspicious return behaviors. However, it is crucial to verify the feasibility and legality of such a policy within the establishment, ensuring alignment with company regulations and legal requirements.

Before adopting this practice, it is recommended to conduct a thorough assessment to determine if requiring ID aligns with the established norms, company policies, and local laws. This proactive approach ensures that the implementation of this measure is not only effective in deterring fraudulent returns but also compliant with relevant legal and regulatory frameworks.

Employee Theft

While trusting employees is essential for a positive work environment, safeguarding against internal theft is a prudent practice for retailers. Proper preparation and awareness are crucial, considering that employee theft constitutes a substantial proportion of significant losses incurred by businesses.

Employee theft can manifest in various forms, extending beyond conventional notions of simple merchandise theft.

Some notable forms include:

Simple Theft of Merchandise: Direct appropriation of goods by employees.

Linking Fake Returns and Fraudulent Gift Cards: Unscrupulous practices involving false returns leading to the issuance of fraudulent gift cards.

"Friendships" and Misuse of Employee Discounts: Instances where employees may selectively forget to scan items for friends or family members or misuse their employee discount privileges.

Embezzlement from Cashiers: Covert embezzlement of money from cashiers, often executed in small increments over time, which cumulatively results in substantial losses.

While acknowledging the importance of trust within the workplace, implementing measures to prevent and detect employee theft is a responsible and necessary aspect of loss prevention. Establishing clear policies, conducting regular audits, and fostering a culture of integrity can collectively contribute to minimizing the risk of losses due to internal theft.

Fraud two sellers

This category of fraud constitutes a relatively low percentage and can be delineated into two distinct methods:

Product Verification and Billing: Fraudulent activities encompassing the verification and billing processes, wherein individuals manipulate product details to deceive the system.

Employee Theft during Checks:

Instances where employees pilfer materials during routine checks, leveraging opportunities to discreetly remove products without arousing suspicion.

Direct In-Store Thefts by Third Parties

The methodologies employed in direct thefts within stores vary based on factors such as location, the presence of security systems, foot traffic in stores, employee types, and other influencing elements.

Some common tactics include:

Concealing Products in Shopping Carts: Offenders covertly hide products within shopping carts to evade detection.

Exchange of Boxes with Other Products: Perpetrators swap product boxes, replacing them with different items to mislead surveillance.

Utilizing Changing Rooms to Conceal Stolen Items: Offenders bring stolen items into changing rooms, wearing pieces to conceal the pilfered merchandise.

These tactics are just a few examples among the myriad cases of direct theft, each uniquely influenced by the specific characteristics of the store environment. Factors such as security systems, employee vigilance, and the flow of people in the store contribute to the diversification of theft methodologies.

Security culture is not "Private security" is security promoted by everyone for all

Foundations of Store Risk: A Comprehensive Study and Analysis

Conducting a comprehensive study and analysis of risks in any establishment requires a meticulous approach, with key considerations extending beyond the realm of security professionals. While security expertise is valuable, individuals from various backgrounds can engage in this process by focusing on critical aspects. Two pivotal components, the Internal Context and External Context, stand out as essential facets in both the risk analysis process and overall operational strategy.

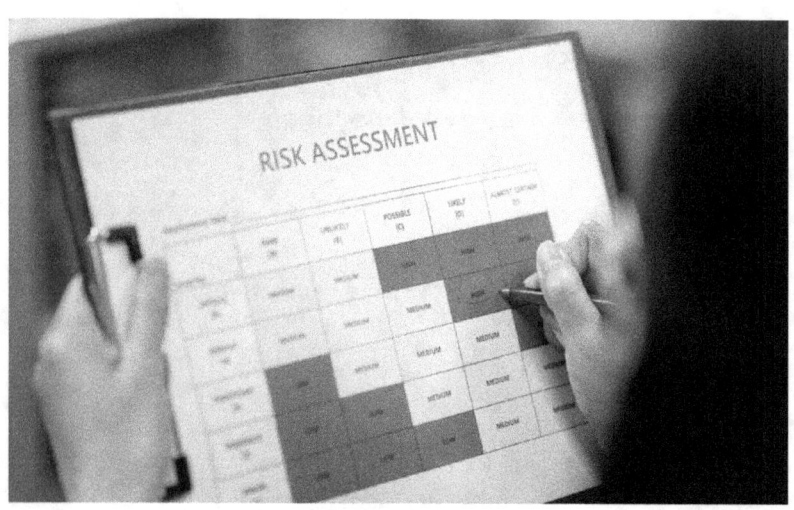

Internal Context: This encompasses the internal dynamics, operations, and factors within the establishment. Key aspects include:

Physical Layout and Infrastructure:

Assessing the layout of the store, including entrances, exits, and vulnerable areas, is crucial. Understanding the infrastructure aids in identifying potential security vulnerabilities.

Employee Dynamics:

Examining the employee structure, their roles, responsibilities, and levels of access contributes to understanding internal security risks. Awareness of staff dynamics is essential for mitigating internal threats.

Inventory Management:

An in-depth analysis of inventory management practices helps identify potential areas of concern, such as discrepancies in stock levels, which may indicate internal theft or procedural issues.

Security Protocols: Reviewing existing security protocols and measures in place provides insights into the current state of security readiness.

External Context: This pertains to external factors that can impact the store's security and operations. Key considerations include:

Location and Surroundings: Evaluating the geographical location and surroundings of the store helps gauge external threats, such as crime rates in the area or proximity to high-risk zones.

Community and Customer Profile: Understanding the demographic and behavioral aspects of the local community and customer base aids in tailoring security measures to specific needs and potential risks.

Local Regulations and Compliance: Familiarizing oneself with local regulations and compliance requirements ensures that security measures align with legal standards and industry norms.

External Threat Landscape: Monitoring external threats, including trends in criminal activities, helps anticipate potential risks and allows for proactive security measures.

Engaging in a basic study of these internal and external contexts lays the foundation for a robust risk analysis. It empowers stakeholders, regardless of their professional background, to contribute meaningfully to the establishment's security strategy and overall risk management.

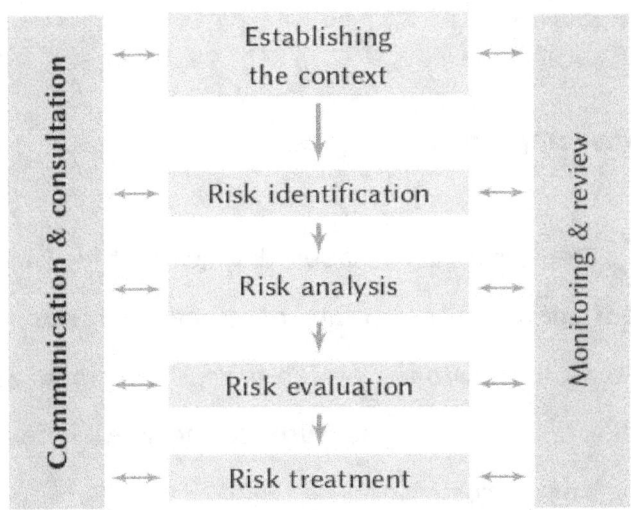

Enhancing Understanding of Customer Context through Collaborative Approaches

Before embarking on any Site Security Assessment or establishing a security culture, recognizing the customer context is paramount. Seeking assistance from various departments within the company is instrumental in gaining valuable insights. Departments such as Marketing, Finance, Purchasing, and others routinely conduct studies that can significantly inform our security endeavors.

Collaborative Approach:

Marketing Department: Collaborating with the Marketing Department allows us to tap into consumer behavior studies, market trends, and customer preferences. Understanding these factors helps tailor security measures to the specific needs and expectations of the customer base.

Finance Department: The Finance Department often conducts financial analyses and risk assessments. Leveraging their insights enables us to align security strategies with the financial well-being of the company, ensuring a judicious allocation of resources.

Purchasing Department: Insights from the Purchasing Department shed light on the supply chain and vendor relationships. Understanding these aspects is crucial for identifying potential vulnerabilities and fortifying security measures throughout the procurement process.

Teamwork in Action:

Let's delve into an exemplary tool for understanding the external context – the PEST Analysis.

PEST Analysis

PEST (Political, Economic, Social, Technological) analysis is a comprehensive model designed to facilitate an in-depth understanding of external factors influencing companies' operations. By expanding to PESTEL (Political, Economic, Social, Technological, Environmental, Legal) Analysis, we broaden our fact-finding endeavors to encompass a more exhaustive range of external considerations.

Political Factors: Evaluate the impact of political factors such as government policies, regulations, and stability on security considerations.

Economic Factors: Examine economic factors like inflation rates, economic growth, and currency fluctuations to align security measures with financial realities.

Social Factors: Understand societal trends, demographics, and cultural influences to tailor security strategies that resonate with the community and customer base.

Technological Factors: Assess technological advancements and trends to ensure security measures are in sync with the evolving technological landscape.

Environmental Factors: Consider environmental factors such as sustainability and climate-related risks, which may influence security strategies.

Legal Factors: Scrutinize legal aspects, including regulations and compliance requirements, to ensure security practices adhere to legal standards.

Embracing a collaborative approach and leveraging tools like the PESTEL Analysis not only enriches the Site Security Assessment process but also establishes a foundation for a proactive and adaptive security culture within the organization.

Consider, for instance, the social factor – a change in policy or cultural dynamics may elicit a widespread response from specific age groups, racial communities, or various demographics. This could potentially lead to tensions, riots, strikes, or more aggressive demonstrations, thereby altering our context and posing a threat to facility safety.

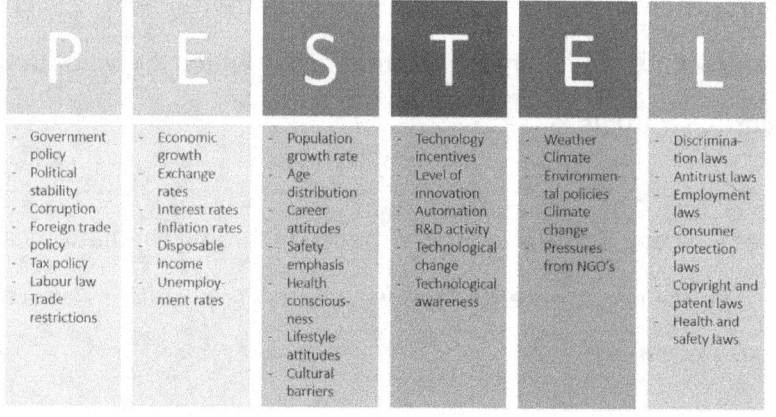

P	E	S	T	E	L
- Government policy	- Economic growth	- Population growth rate	- Technology incentives	- Weather	- Discrimination laws
- Political stability	- Exchange rates	- Age distribution	- Level of innovation	- Climate	- Antitrust laws
- Corruption	- Interest rates	- Career attitudes	- Automation	- Environmental policies	- Employment laws
- Foreign trade policy	- Inflation rates	- Safety emphasis	- R&D activity	- Climate change	- Consumer protection laws
- Tax policy	- Disposable income	- Health consciousness	- Technological change	- Pressures from NGO's	- Copyright and patent laws
- Labour law	- Unemployment rates	- Lifestyle attitudes	- Technological awareness		- Health and safety laws
- Trade restrictions		- Cultural barriers			

A pertinent illustration is found in the Black Lives Matter demonstrations, where we witnessed a surge in violence, incidents of looting, theft, and vandalization. It is crucial to recognize that many owners of establishments, shops, hotels, and restaurants may not have conducted a risk analysis based on such events, often assuming that such occurrences are unlikely.

Swot Analysis:

SWOT (Strengths, Weaknesses, Opportunities, Threats) Analysis is a strategic planning tool that plays a pivotal role in assessing and managing risks within a security framework. While traditionally associated with business and organizational strategy, its application extends seamlessly to the realm of security assessments. Understanding the significance of SWOT in the context of security is crucial for developing effective risk management strategies and fortifying security measures.

Strengths (S): In the context of security, strengths encompass the internal attributes and capabilities that enhance an organization's ability to mitigate risks and safeguard its assets. This could include robust access control systems, well-trained security personnel, or state-of-the-art surveillance technology. Identifying and leveraging these strengths is essential for building a resilient security infrastructure.

Weaknesses (W): Weaknesses refer to internal vulnerabilities that may expose an organization to security threats. This could range from outdated security protocols to insufficient training programs for staff. Recognizing and addressing these weaknesses is crucial to shoring up potential vulnerabilities and enhancing overall security resilience.

Opportunities (O): Opportunities, in the security context, are external factors that can be leveraged to enhance security measures. This might include advancements in security technology, collaborations with law enforcement, or emerging best practices in the industry. Identifying and capitalizing on these opportunities is integral to staying ahead of potential threats.

Threats (T): Threats encompass external factors that pose risks to an organization's security. These could be anything from geopolitical instability to cyber threats or natural disasters. A thorough analysis of threats is essential for developing proactive strategies to mitigate and respond to potential risks.

Importance in Security Assessment

Holistic Understanding: SWOT provides a comprehensive and structured framework for understanding both internal and external factors that influence security. This holistic perspective enables security professionals to identify potential gaps and strengths in their security posture.

Strategic Planning: By conducting a SWOT analysis, security teams can develop strategic plans that align with the organization's broader objectives. This ensures that security measures are not isolated but integrated into the overall business strategy.

Risk Mitigation: SWOT helps in identifying potential risks and vulnerabilities, allowing organizations to proactively implement measures to mitigate these risks. This can include investing in new technologies, enhancing training programs, or revising security protocols.

Resource Allocation: Understanding strengths and weaknesses assists in the effective allocation of resources. It helps organizations prioritize investments in areas where they are most vulnerable and optimize resources for maximum impact on security.

Adaptability: The dynamic nature of security threats requires organizations to be adaptable. SWOT analysis facilitates an ongoing and adaptive approach to security, allowing for continuous improvement based on changing circumstances.

incorporating SWOT analysis into security assessments provides a structured and strategic framework for organizations to identify, assess, and respond to security risks. It empowers security professionals to develop proactive strategies, enhance resilience, and align security measures with broader organizational goals.

SWOT ANALYSIS

	Helpful to achieving the objective	Harmful to achieving the objective
Internal origin (attributes of the organization)	Strengths	Weaknesses
External origin (attributes of the environment)	Opportunities	Threats

This is the example of a simple system designed to position or verify the strategic position of the company/institution in the environment in question.

The SWOT analysis technique was developed by American Albert Humphrey during the development of a research project at Stanford University between the 1960s and 1970s, using data from Fortune 500, a magazine that makes up a ranking of the largest American companies.

So as security consultants we can and should use this matrix to assist us in a quick assessment of the state of the company's security. We will not solve problems with this matrix, but we can have a quick analysis of the company on the state of security of an area, a site, a critical installation, and others.

SWOT Analysis Example

Fitness and Apparel Store in a Remote Area

In the context of establishing a fitness and apparel store in a remote area, conducting a SWOT analysis becomes a crucial exercise to evaluate the venture's strengths, weaknesses, opportunities, and threats. This strategic planning tool allows for a comprehensive assessment of both internal and external factors that can impact the success of the business.

By delving into the unique challenges and advantages presented by a remote location, the SWOT analysis serves as a valuable framework to make informed decisions and formulate effective strategies.

This exercise aids in uncovering insights that can shape the business model, optimize resources, and navigate the distinct dynamics of operating in an isolated market.

Strengths:

Limited Access Points:

The store's strategic location with controlled entry and exit from the main road provides a natural advantage in terms of access control.

Solid Building Structure:

The robust construction of the building, particularly reinforced entry points, contributes to a strong physical security foundation.

CCTV Coverage:

The presence of CCTV cameras covering key areas enhances surveillance capabilities, deterring potential security threats.

Trained Security Personnel:

Having trained security personnel during operating hours adds a layer of human security, providing a visible deterrent.

Restricted Employee Access:

Limited access to storage areas and the implementation of an electronic key card system contribute to internal security.

Weaknesses:

Limited Visibility:

The remote location with limited foot traffic may result in reduced visibility, potentially enabling unauthorized activities.

Potential Response Challenges:

The secluded surroundings may pose challenges for immediate response in case of incidents, especially during non-peak hours.

Staffing Levels:

Inadequate staffing during non-peak hours may leave the store vulnerable, requiring consideration for 24/7 security coverage.

Lack of Advanced Employee Training:

While basic security training is provided, there's a potential weakness in the absence of advanced training for crisis management and emergency response.

Limited Anti-Shoplifting Measures:

The current measures for high-value merchandise may be insufficient; consideration of electronic article surveillance (EAS) systems is needed.

Opportunities:

Electronic Article Surveillance (EAS):

Implementing EAS systems for high-value merchandise presents an opportunity to enhance anti-shoplifting measures.

Advanced Employee Training:

Providing advanced training for crisis management and emergency response can better prepare staff for unforeseen events.

Expanded Surveillance Coverage:

Enhancing CCTV coverage in blind spots can improve overall surveillance capabilities, reducing vulnerabilities.

Threats:

Potential Unauthorized Activities:

The secluded location poses a potential threat of unauthorized activities due to limited visibility and less frequent foot traffic.

Emergency Preparedness:

Inadequate emergency preparedness measures may lead to challenges during unforeseen events, potentially impacting customer and staff safety.

Conclusion and Recommendations:

To capitalize on its strengths and address weaknesses, the store should consider expanding surveillance coverage, investing in employee training for crisis management, and exploring the implementation of EAS systems. Additionally, conducting regular emergency drills and assessing the feasibility of 24/7 security coverage during low-traffic hours will contribute to a more robust security posture.

Adjustments and improvements based on ongoing assessments will help the store adapt to evolving security needs in its unique and remote setting.

As store managers, loss prevention specialists, risk management professionals, or individuals in any capacity influencing the operational processes of these establishments, it is imperative to possess comprehensive knowledge of SWOT analyses. These analyses offer a nuanced understanding of the internal and external factors that directly impact the security and risk landscape of the business.

Understanding the internal context involves recognizing the inherent strengths and weaknesses of the establishment. For instance, acknowledging the limited access points and the robust building structure can empower managers to leverage these strengths for enhanced security. Simultaneously, recognizing weaknesses such as potential response challenges during non-peak hours prompts the formulation of targeted strategies to address vulnerabilities.

On the external front, identifying opportunities and threats is equally critical. Opportunities, like implementing Electronic Article Surveillance (EAS) systems, can significantly bolster anti-shoplifting measures. Conversely, acknowledging threats, such as the potential for unauthorized activities due to the remote location, allows for proactive measures to mitigate risks.

This comprehension of the internal and external landscape is paramount, as it directly influences decision-making processes. Whether it involves designing security protocols, allocating resources, or implementing loss prevention strategies, a nuanced understanding of the SWOT analysis can necessitate adjustments or even a complete overhaul of existing projects.

Failure to integrate these analyses into the decision-making framework may result in suboptimal security measures that inadequately address the specific challenges and opportunities posed by the store's unique context.

In essence, a general awareness of SWOT analyses empowers stakeholders to make informed decisions, adapt strategies to the dynamic security environment, and ultimately contribute to the overall resilience and success of the establishment.

Radio communications

Enhancing Retail Security through Effective Radio Communications

In the retail environment, effective communication is paramount, and radio communication stands out as one of the most utilized tools among various departments, including support staff, sales teams, and internal management. However, it is crucial to recognize that customer-facing communication should remain discreet, employing an internal code with specific expressions for various scenarios.

Establishing an Internal Code: Creating an internal code with specific references is instrumental in maintaining a secure and efficient communication system within the store.

This code should encompass distinct expressions for different occurrences, individuals, potential security threats, or known criminals who may have been exposed in the store. This internal language ensures that sensitive information is conveyed without compromising security measures.

Radio Communication Rules:

Sequential Communication:

Unlike phone communication, a two-way radio requires sequential talking and listening. This distinction is critical for clear and effective exchanges.

Non-Interruptive Protocol:

It is imperative not to interrupt ongoing conversations unless it is an emergency. Emergency messages should be clearly conveyed, respecting ongoing communications.

Discerning Responses:

Only respond to radio calls if certain that they pertain to your role or responsibilities, ensuring efficient and focused communication.

Confidentiality Guidelines:

Strictly avoid transmitting confidential, financial, or military information over the radio to maintain the integrity of sensitive data.

Secure Conversations:

Unless conversations are encrypted at an appropriate level, assume they can be overheard. Exercise caution when discussing sensitive matters over the radio.

Equipment Maintenance:

Regularly conduct radio checks to ensure equipment functionality, including battery status, power, and reception range.

Volume and Clarity:

Maintain an audible volume level to ensure calls are heard, and periodically perform radio checks to validate equipment integrity.

Call Signals and Locations:

Memorize call signals and locations associated with regular communication partners, streamlining interactions for efficiency.

Anonymous Communication:

In radio communication, individuals are identified by call signals rather than names, reinforcing a secure and discreet communication environment.

Thoughtful Communication:

Prioritize thoughtful communication, considering the content and intended recipient before speaking.

Conciseness and Clarity:

Keep conversations concise, accurate, and clear, avoiding unnecessarily lengthy or complicated sentences.

Abbreviation Awareness:

Exercise caution with abbreviations, ensuring they are universally understood within the group to prevent misinterpretation.

Implementing and adhering to these rules and guidelines for radio communication ensures that the retail environment maintains a secure, efficient, and discreet means of conveying vital information among staff members, ultimately contributing to a safer and more organized store operation.

Describing a Potential Crime and Suspect

Enhancing Accuracy in Suspect Descriptions and Incident Reporting

In the realm of crime reporting and investigation, the art of describing a potential crime and its associated suspect is a critical skill. This chapter delves into the intricacies of effectively articulating the details surrounding a potential criminal incident.

From deciphering the elements of a crime scene to providing accurate and comprehensive suspect descriptions, this section aims to equip readers with the necessary tools to convey crucial information to law enforcement professionals. Understanding the nuances of descriptive language, discerning relevant details, and employing a structured approach are key components explored in unraveling the complexities of narrating a possible crime and identifying a suspect. Through practical guidance and illustrative examples, readers will gain insights into the art and science of painting a vivid picture that aids in the swift resolution of criminal cases.

In the aftermath of an incident, providing detailed and accurate descriptions of alleged crimes and suspects is paramount to effective resolution and the overall security of the establishment. Relying on vague or general observations may lead to errors with potentially severe consequences for the company.

Here are essential guidelines for creating precise and realistic suspect descriptions:

Critical Location Information:

Crime Scene Details:

Note the exact location of the crime within the store and any previous encounters with the suspect.

Time and Weapon Identification:

Record the time of the incident and identify any weapons the suspect may possess, specifying the type, such as revolver, shotgun, knife, etc.

Observation of Escape:

If the suspect leaves the scene, carefully observe the direction they take.

Vehicle Information:

If the suspect uses a vehicle, note details like type, color, make, model, state, and registration numbers.

Potential Accomplices:

Be attentive to the presence of observers or colleagues associated with the suspect.

Suspect Description

General Characteristics:

Document the suspect's gender, race, or national origin, estimated age, and physique without resorting to discriminatory language.

Practical Example:

Avoid stereotyping; for instance, refrain from associating a specific ethnicity with criminal behavior.

Specific Facial Features

Hair Details:

Note color, texture, style, and the possibility of dyes or wigs.

Forehead, Eyes, Nose, and Ears:

Observe forehead height, eye color, nose shape, and ear size and prominence.

Mouth, Chin, and Neck:

Document mouth characteristics, chin shape, and any notable features on the neck.

Skin Features:

Note complexion, birthmarks, acne, rashes, or swellings.

Facial Hair and Tattoos:

Describe facial hair, beard style, or tattoos, specifying their location on the body.

Clothing Details

Headwear:

Document hat color, style, ornaments, and how it is worn.

Upper Body:

Describe jacket color, style, and any distinguishing features on shirts, blouses, or dresses.

Lower Body:

Note pants or skirt color, style, and cuffs.

Footwear and Accessories:

Describe shoe color, style, and brand if possible, along with any accessories or jewelry.

Overall Appearance:

Document whether the suspect appears organized or sloppy, clean, or dirty.

Oddities:
Look for unusual clothing sizes, strange colors, or patchwork patterns.

Creating a detailed and accurate suspect description empowers security forces to respond effectively. It is crucial to familiarize oneself with these guidelines and conduct practice exercises among colleagues to ensure proficiency in identifying and reporting suspects based on the outlined points.

This meticulous approach significantly enhances the reliability of incident reports and aids in the swift and accurate resolution of security-related matters.

Instances of Describing a Suspect

Example 1: Caucasian Individual

General Characteristics:

   Gender: Male

   Race: Caucasian

   Age: Approximately mid-30s

   Build: Average build

   Height: Around 5 feet 10 inches

Facial Features:

Hair: Brown, short, neatly groomed

Eyes: Blue, round-shaped

Nose: Straight and medium-sized

Lips: Medium thickness, downturned at the corners

Facial Hair: Clean-shaven

Clothing Details:

Headwear: None

Upper Body: Wearing a navy blue jacket with a small logo on the left chest, light blue collared shirt

Lower Body: Dark blue jeans

Footwear: Brown leather shoes

Accessories: Wearing a silver wristwatch on the left wrist

Overall Appearance:

Clean and well-groomed

Carrying a black backpack

No visible tattoos or distinctive marks

Example 2: Black Individual

General Characteristics:

Gender: Female

Race: Black

Age: Approximately early 20s

Build: Slim

Height: Around 5 feet 6 inches

Facial Features:

Hair: Natural, black, medium-length afro

Eyes: Brown, almond-shaped

Nose: Small and slightly broad

Lips: Full and symmetrical

Clothing Details:

Headwear: Wearing a patterned headwrap

Upper Body: Pink hoodie with a graphic design, black leggings

Lower Body: Black ankle boots

Accessories: Silver hoop earrings, a small silver pendant necklace

Overall Appearance:

    Casual and trendy style

    Carrying a small black shoulder bag

    No visible tattoos or distinctive marks

Remember, it's essential to focus on observable and relevant details without making assumptions or using discriminatory language. Descriptions should remain neutral and free from stereotypes to ensure fairness and accuracy.

Methods for Detaining a Suspect

Detaining a suspect is a critical process that demands a careful and lawful approach, whether in the context of security in a retail setting or civilian involvement. In both scenarios, it's essential to prioritize safety, follow legal guidelines, and act responsibly to prevent any escalation. This section will explore methods for detaining a suspect, addressing key considerations for security personnel and civilians alike.

Security Retail Perspective

Assessment and Identification:

Security personnel should undergo thorough training to accurately assess situations and identify potential suspects. Utilize surveillance systems, CCTV cameras, and other monitoring tools to gather evidence and make informed decisions.

Effective Communication:

Before taking any action, security personnel must communicate clearly and authoritatively, informing the suspect of the reason for detainment.

Effective verbal communication skills are crucial to avoid misunderstandings and maintain control over the situation.

Legal Understanding:

Security professionals must have a comprehensive understanding of local laws regarding citizen's arrest and detainment. Adherence to legal procedures is vital to prevent any legal repercussions for both the security personnel and the establishment.

Collaboration with Law Enforcement:

If a suspect is detained, security personnel should cooperate with law enforcement authorities promptly. Provide accurate information and any evidence gathered to assist in the legal process.

Civilian Perspective

Prioritize Personal Safety:

Civilians should prioritize personal safety and avoid confrontations whenever possible. Only consider detainment if there's an immediate threat to personal safety or the safety of others.

Observation and Documentation:

If witnessing a potential crime, civilians should focus on observing details about the suspect and the situation. Document relevant information, such as appearance, behavior, and any identifying features.

Contacting Authorities:

Instead of attempting to detain a suspect personally, civilians should contact law enforcement immediately. Provide a clear and detailed description of the situation and the suspect.

Non-Confrontational Approach:

If it becomes necessary to interact with the suspect, civilians should maintain a non-confrontational demeanor. Avoid using force unless necessary for self-defense.

Legal Awareness:

Civilians should be aware of the legal implications of attempting to detain a suspect.

Understand the laws in the jurisdiction and act within the confines of legal boundaries.

In conclusion, whether in a retail security or civilian context, the methods for detaining a suspect should prioritize safety, effective communication, legal adherence, and collaboration with law enforcement.

It is crucial to approach such situations with a level-headed and responsible mindset to ensure a lawful and secure resolution.

While the law permits such detentions, complications may arise when a suspect is aware of their legal rights, and law enforcement is occupied or delayed. Extended detentions could lead to claims of false imprisonment. To address this, it is crucial to exercise experience and follow proper procedures. Confirming the suspect's identity, linking them to the stolen items, and ensuring the legal basis for the detention are essential steps.

In situations where suspects may be aware of surveillance, it becomes imperative to secure evidence and prevent potential interference with stolen items.

Global Comment on Detaining Suspects

Legal Foundation in Accordance with Each Country's Laws

It is imperative to underscore that any act of detaining a suspect must be firmly grounded in the legal framework of the respective country. Laws pertaining to the arrest, detention, and handling of suspects vary significantly across jurisdictions, reflecting cultural, political, and social nuances.

In the absence of comprehensive knowledge about the legal intricacies of every country, it is a fundamental principle that any detention of a suspect should strictly adhere to the laws and regulations of the specific jurisdiction in question. This necessitates a nuanced understanding of local statutes, criminal procedure codes, and human rights provisions that govern such actions.

Individuals entrusted with the responsibility of apprehending suspects must be well-versed in the legal landscape of their jurisdiction.

This includes a clear understanding of the circumstances under which a suspect can be detained, the requisite procedures for arrest, and the rights afforded to the detained individual.

Furthermore, considerations such as the presumption of innocence until proven guilty, due process, and protection of individual liberties must be upheld in accordance with the laws of the land. A failure to adhere to these legal principles can result in severe consequences, including legal challenges, reputational damage, and potential violations of human rights.

In summary, any act of detainment should be conducted with a meticulous commitment to the legal protocols and standards specific to the country in which it occurs. It is incumbent upon those involved in law enforcement or security to continuously update their knowledge of local laws to ensure the proper and lawful execution of their responsibilities.

Fake money-making

Managing Cash Flow in Retail Stores: Detecting, Avoiding, and Controlling Financial Vulnerabilities

In the dynamic landscape of retail, managing cash flow effectively is paramount to the financial health and security of a store. Cash transactions inherently pose unique challenges, making it crucial for retail establishments to adopt proactive measures to detect, avoid, and control potential risks. As a security expert, addressing these financial vulnerabilities requires a multi-faceted approach:

Detection of Vulnerabilities:

Conduct Regular Audits: Implement routine financial audits to identify discrepancies, irregularities, or potential loopholes in cash handling procedures.

Utilize Technology: Employ advanced point-of-sale (POS) systems and surveillance technologies that provide real-time monitoring and transaction tracking.

Avoidance of Risks:

Cashless Transactions: Encourage and promote cashless transactions to minimize the volume of physical cash on-site, reducing the risk of theft.

Employee Training: Invest in comprehensive training programs for staff to enhance their awareness of potential risks and emphasize adherence to secure cash-handling protocols.

Control Measures:

Secure Cash Handling Protocols: Establish and enforce strict protocols for handling, transporting, and depositing cash. This includes limiting access to cash to only authorized personnel.

Cash Safes and Depositories: Install secure safes and depositories that deter unauthorized access and provide an additional layer of protection for cash assets.

Implement Cash Limits: Enforce limitations on the amount of cash that can be kept on-site, reducing the potential loss in the event of theft.

Surveillance and Security Systems:

Strategic Camera Placement: Install surveillance cameras strategically, covering all cash-handling points, entry and exit points, and areas with high cash traffic.

Alarm Systems: Implement robust alarm systems that can detect unauthorized access, breaches, or unusual activities, triggering immediate responses.

Employee Integrity Measures:

Background Checks: Conduct thorough background checks on employees involved in cash handling to ensure a level of trustworthiness and reliability.

Rotate Responsibilities: Implement periodic rotation of cash-handling responsibilities among staff to mitigate the risk of collusion or internal theft.

Collaborate with Financial Institutions:

Armored Transport Services: Consider utilizing armored transport services for cash deposits and transfers to external locations, ensuring secure and monitored transportation.

Bank Partnerships: Establish strong relationships with financial institutions to facilitate timely deposits, reducing the amount of cash stored on-site.

As a security expert, it is crucial to continually assess and adapt these measures to the evolving landscape of retail security. By adopting a comprehensive approach that combines technology, procedural rigor, and employee training, retail stores can effectively manage financial risks and fortify their defenses against potential vulnerabilities.

Counter measures

Detecting fake money is a critical aspect of managing cash transactions in retail stores. Here are some technologies and techniques that store managers and staff can employ in their daily operations to identify counterfeit currency:

UV (Ultraviolet) Lamps:

Comment: UV lamps are effective in revealing security features embedded in legitimate banknotes. Genuine currency often includes UV-reactive elements that are not present in counterfeit bills.

Counterfeit Detection Pens:

Comment: Counterfeit detection pens contain a special ink that reacts differently with genuine and counterfeit banknotes. Store staff can quickly mark a bill, and the reaction of the ink helps determine its authenticity.

Currency Sorting Machines:

Comment: Automated currency sorting machines equipped with counterfeit detection features can streamline the process of identifying fake bills. These machines use various technologies, including UV, infrared, and magnetic sensors.

Magnifying Tools:

Comment: Magnifying glasses or microscopes can help examine intricate details on banknotes, such as fine lines, microprinting, and watermarks, which are often difficult for counterfeiters to replicate.

Mobile Apps for Counterfeit Detection:

Comment: Some mobile applications use the smartphone's camera to analyze and verify the authenticity of banknotes. These apps often provide real-time feedback on security features.

Infrared (IR) Sensors:

Comment: Infrared sensors can detect specific features, such as infrared ink, present in genuine banknotes but absent in counterfeit currency. IR technology adds an extra layer of security for cash handlers.

Holographic Features:

Comment: Genuine banknotes may incorporate holographic features, such as holographic stripes or patches. Counterfeiters find it challenging to replicate these holograms accurately.

High-Resolution Scanners:

Comment: High-resolution scanners can be used to capture detailed images of banknotes, enabling staff to examine intricate features and detect irregularities.

Magnetic Ink Detection:

Comment: Some currencies use magnetic ink in specific areas. Magnetic detectors can identify the magnetic properties of ink, helping to distinguish genuine notes from counterfeit ones.

Educational Training Programs:

Comment: Regular training programs for store staff on the latest security features of currency can be invaluable.

This ensures that employees are aware of the latest counterfeiting techniques and can stay vigilant.

Central Bank Guidelines:

Comment: Familiarizing staff with the guidelines provided by the central bank regarding security features on currency notes is essential. Central banks often release educational materials and guidelines to help businesses identify genuine notes.

Internet Resources and Updates:

Comment: Staying informed about the latest trends in counterfeiting through online resources, central bank updates, and law enforcement agencies can empower store managers and staff to recognize new threats.

By combining these technologies and training methods, retail stores can establish a robust system for detecting counterfeit money, protecting their assets, and maintaining the integrity of financial transactions.

Navigating Testimony: A Guide for Legal Settings and Law Enforcement Interactions

Reporting a crime to the police is a crucial step for various reasons, including seeking protection, recovering assets, preventing further victimization, and facilitating insurance claims or involving security companies.

In Portugal, as well as globally, understanding the process of testifying in court or at police stations is essential for individuals and businesses.

Reasons to Involve the Police: There are situations where individuals or employees may hesitate to involve the police due to fears of retaliation, especially when the perpetrator is known to them. In such cases, seeking assistance from others to report the crime can be considered. It is important to recognize that involving the security forces promptly enhances the chances of preserving evidence and apprehending the offender.

Police Involvement: Upon reporting a crime, the police may either visit the crime scene or require individuals to go to the police station to provide a detailed account. In emergency situations, the police take immediate steps to protect those in distress or secure the premises, especially in cases involving violence or firearms. The collection and preservation of evidence are critical aspects of their response, potentially leading to restricted access to the crime scene temporarily.

Making Statements: When reporting a crime, individuals are typically asked to provide a comprehensive statement to the police. An officer will interview the person, asking detailed questions about the incident. It is crucial to disclose all relevant information, and the statement may be written by the individual or transcribed by the police for verification. Individuals should carefully review and sign the statement, with the option to request a copy.

Recording Statements: In certain cases, statements may be recorded for future reference or testimonials. Individuals may be nervous or anxious during this process, and it is vital to ensure the accuracy and completeness of the statement. A thorough and accurate account of the incident is essential for effective law enforcement and potential legal proceedings.

Witness Testimony: If the alleged criminal is apprehended and a trial ensues, the individual providing the statement may be called as a witness.

As a witness, one may undergo questioning by the defense based on the information provided in the statement. Therefore, the accuracy and clarity of the initial statement become pivotal during legal proceedings.

Understanding the procedures involved in testifying in court, at police stations, or to police officers is essential for individuals and businesses alike. Cooperation with law enforcement authorities ensures the thorough investigation of crimes and contributes to the overall safety and security of the community.

Terminology

In every profession and sector, specific terminology is used to communicate effectively within the industry. This holds true for various companies, economic groups, and sectors, each having its own set of terms and phrases. Here, we will explore some international terms that can be adapted to the context in Portugal.

SHRINK - Discrepancies

Discrepancy refers to the loss of stock that can be attributed to factors such as employee theft, shoplifting, administrative errors, supplier fraud, damages, and cash errors. It represents the variance between the stock recorded in a company's balance sheet or Customer Relationship Management (CRM) system and its actual stock.

This concept poses a significant challenge for managers and shopkeepers as it leads to the loss of stock, ultimately resulting in a decrease in profits.

Key Terms:

Discrepancy: Describes the depletion of inventory caused by store robberies, fraudulent sellers, employee thefts, human errors, and mismanagement.

Difference: The variance between the recorded inventory and the current inventory is measured by the term "discrepancy."

Loss of Profits: The consequence of the discrepancy is a reduction in profits due to the unsold inventories purchased.

Controlling Discrepancy:

To mitigate the impact of discrepancies, management should conduct regular inventory audits, implement Closed-Circuit Television (CCTV) systems, monitor the activities of sellers, and provide awareness training to employees. The prevention of discrepancies is crucial, considering the substantial annual losses incurred by companies in this sector. Urgent investments in security policies and a safety culture are imperative to address these challenges effectively.

External Thefts

Individuals involved in illicit activities, commonly known as offenders or perpetrators, deliberately take risks within stores daily to steal products for personal consumption or to resell in the underground market.

Internal Theft:

Theft and losses orchestrated by personnel within the company, including sales staff, cleaning crews, security personnel, or any employee with access to the store premises.

Casual Shoplifter: Individuals who engage in theft for personal use, targeting a specific product without any intention of paying for it, driven by various motivations such as thrill-seeking or financial constraints.

Organized Retail Robber: Individuals who adopt shoplifting as a consistent means of livelihood, stealing specific products with the intent to resell them. This lifestyle choice is often observed in individuals with dependencies like drug addicts looking to fund their habits.

Favored — Sliding: A scenario where a company employee releases merchandise without receiving payment within the store, creating a system to discreetly provide products to a friend or family member while internally concealing their actions.

Observer: An individual who meticulously examines the store, identifying its security system, vulnerabilities, and subsequently relaying this information to a potential thief or an organized theft group.

Went Red: An expression used when an individual who has stolen a product from the store is identified and appears to be preparing to flee without completing the payment. These expressions are crafted by the security manager and should undergo regular changes to maintain their efficacy.

Electrician: A term used to discreetly request the presence of security without arousing suspicion. When contacting the police via radio or phone, the use of such terminology ensures a covert communication that avoids jeopardizing the situation and alerting potential wrongdoers.

Shadow Shopper: An individual who subtly moves around the store, mimicking a regular shopper but with the intention of identifying blind spots, vulnerable areas, or weaknesses in the security system for potential theft or future illegal activities.

Ghost Customer: A person who enters the store under the guise of a genuine customer but is secretly surveying the layout, security measures, and staff behavior for ulterior motives, including aiding future theft attempts.

Panic Patron: Someone who intentionally creates chaos or distractions within the store, diverting attention from their accomplices who may be engaging in theft. This can involve staged disturbances, fake emergencies, or disruptive behavior.

Routine Robber: Individuals who meticulously study the store's daily routines, staff shifts, and security patterns to plan thefts during specific timeframes when they believe they can exploit weaknesses in surveillance.

Crafty Collaborator: An employee or insider who collaborates with external thieves, providing critical information, such as inventory details, security vulnerabilities, or optimal times for theft, in exchange for a share of the stolen goods or monetary compensation.

Introduction to the safety of shopkeepers

Introduction to Shopkeeper Safety Management

As directors, managers, supervisors, or even store guards, it is imperative to develop a comprehensive training program for the entire collective staff working in stores. This includes managers, employees, interns, cleaning staff, and all other personnel associated with the establishment.

Creating an effective training program is crucial, ensuring that it covers essential topics in a practical and assertive manner. Despite the potential lack of interest in safety from some employees, it is vital to convey that failures in safety measures directly and indirectly affect them.

The foundational training for shopkeepers encompasses a broad spectrum of knowledge, covering aspects related to administration, finance, sales, customer service, and inventory management.

The following key skills and knowledge areas are essential for shopkeepers:

Administration: Basic understanding of business management, strategic planning, budgeting, and accounting.

Finance: Proficiency in controlling cash flow, personal and business finance management, inventory management, and cost and expense control.

Sales: Knowledge of sales techniques, customer service, customer loyalty, negotiation, and marketing.

Customer Service: Communication skills, empathy, effective problem-solving, conflict resolution, and the ability to provide excellent customer service.

Stock Management: Understanding inventory control techniques, prevention of loss and theft, merchandise organization, supply chain management, replenishment, and inventory.

Leadership: Leadership skills to motivate and manage a team of employees, task delegation, conflict management, talent development, and goal setting.

Beyond these fundamental skills, it is crucial for shopkeepers to stay updated on market trends and industry news. Having an entrepreneurial mindset is essential for seizing business opportunities that may arise over time. Continuous learning and skill improvement through courses, lectures, and workshops are highly recommended.

This manual and training will specifically address the integration of daily tasks with a focus on supporting the safety and loss management of the establishment.

Processes and Strategies for Loss Prevention in Retail

Initiating our journey with a focus on process optimization, dedicated teams in sales and process management collaborate to enhance the company's efficiency.

The primary objectives include:

Control Losses by Improving Inventory Results

Increase Sales to Improve Overall Profitability

Introduction to Theft Typologies

Understanding the typologies of thefts within the social context and market segment is pivotal. This involves exploring various theft types, methods, techniques, and common practices. It's crucial to recognize that loss prevention extends beyond averting shoplifting incidents, encompassing a comprehensive set of processes and measures.

Defensive and Offensive Posture

Every person entering a store is initially a customer, emphasizing the need for a dual defensive and offensive posture. To combat, prevent, and reduce diverse forms of losses, employees must remain vigilant, even during busy or distracted moments.

Procedures for Day-to-Day Tasks

Entrance and Exit Supervision:

Entrances and exits require continuous supervision to ensure fluidity and the establishment's safety. If leaving one's post, colleagues should keep entry and exit points within sight.

Staff Location and Surveillance:

Ensure 360% vision coverage of all store areas by co-workers and CCTV systems. Pay special attention to preferred, profitable, and trending articles.

Effective Communication:

Establish a code list for specific situations to ensure uniqueness in message contents.

Provider Management Procedures:

Closed doors/curtains open.

Thoroughly check items, damage, labels, and alarms.

Verify the tester before customer entry.

Maintain visual contact with the tester during customer interaction.

Check items on the way out.

Inspect the tester after the customer's departure.

Alarms in Anti-Theft Antennas

Addressing alarms on anti-theft antennas requires careful consideration. Factors triggering alarms may range from deactivated male alarms on product bags from other stores to stolen material.

Approaching customers in such situations demands cordiality, a smile, and clear communication.

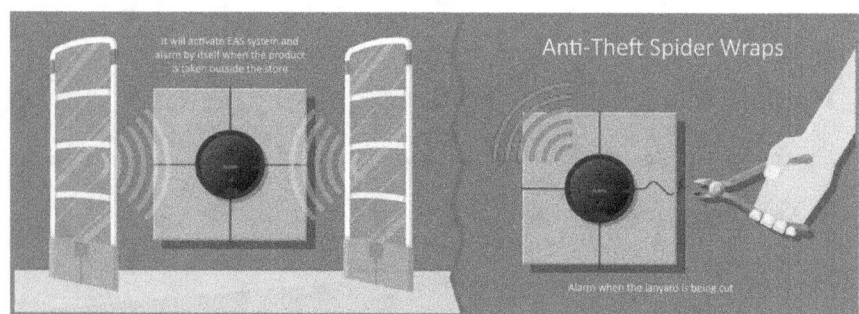

External Thefts

Explore various typologies of external thefts, including simple theft, group theft, swipe of opportunity, counterfeiting, parcel theft, cargo theft, return fraud, theft in warehouses, and ATM theft. Techniques used involve concealment, hidden bags, aluminum-lined bags, baby cars, disarming alarms, and going over antennas.

Fraud Prevention in Retail Stores

Various types of fraud in retail store transactions include return fraud, exchange fraud, discount fraud, theft of money, credit card fraud, gift card fraud, coupon fraud, and sales cancellation fraud. Basic preventive procedures include checking banknotes on detectors, recounting money if customers ask for notes back, and utilizing CCTV for verification.

Management and Control of Goods under Loss Prevention

The procedures for the management and control of goods in retail stores under loss prevention aim to reduce losses from theft, breakage, damage, operational errors, and fraud. Practices include access control, goods receipt, and issue control, monitoring by cameras, periodic inventory, safety labels, control of returns, employee training, and data analysis.

By adopting these systematic procedures and continuously monitoring and evaluating their effectiveness, retail stores can prevent losses and ensure sustained business profitability.

Internal theft

Commonly known as employee shoplifting, poses a pervasive threat to the financial well-being and integrity of retail businesses. Implementing a multifaceted approach can effectively mitigate such risks:

Comprehensive Employee Screening:

Conduct extensive background checks on potential hires, examining their job history, criminal records, and seeking references from previous employers.

Example: A candidate with a history of theft-related offenses or suspicious employment terminations should raise a red flag during the screening process.

Transparent Theft Policies:

Clearly define and communicate policies regarding theft, emphasizing the company's zero-tolerance stance. Create an organizational culture that places a premium on integrity.

Example: A well-articulated policy may state that any form of theft, including taking home merchandise without proper authorization, will result in immediate termination.

Stringent Stock Control Measures:

Implement robust stock control procedures, including regular stock level monitoring, identifying fast and slow-moving items, and adjusting restocking orders to minimize losses and waste.

Example: By utilizing inventory management software, a retail store can identify patterns of theft or discrepancies between recorded and actual stock levels.

Access Controls:

Restrict access to inventory areas and other sensitive zones, ensuring that only authorized personnel can enter these spaces. Example: Installing keycard access systems or biometric controls can prevent unauthorized entry, limiting the opportunities for internal theft.

Continuous Employee Training:

Conduct ongoing training sessions to educate employees about the importance of loss prevention, providing insights into identifying and reporting suspicious activities.

Example: Role-playing scenarios during training sessions can enhance employees' ability to recognize and respond to potential theft situations.

Employee Activity Monitoring:
Employ security cameras to monitor employee activities, helping to identify and investigate any unusual behavior promptly.
Example: Video footage analysis can reveal patterns of behavior, such as repeatedly visiting certain areas without apparent work-related reasons.

Anonymous Reporting Program:
Establish a confidential reporting mechanism that empowers employees to report suspicious activities without fear of retribution.

Example: An anonymous tip hotline or an online reporting system can encourage employees to come forward with valuable information.

Internal Audit Program:

Implement routine internal audits to scrutinize employee activities, identify deviations, and maintain a proactive stance against internal theft.

Example: Randomized audits of cash registers, inventory, and employee activities can uncover discrepancies and discourage potential theft.

By integrating these strategies into daily operations and emphasizing them in employee training programs, businesses can create a secure environment and fortify their financial integrity against the threat of internal theft.

Let's create a safe environment.

Conclusion:

In the ever-evolving landscape of retail, where challenges such as theft, fraud, and security breaches are prevalent, adopting effective loss prevention strategies becomes paramount. This comprehensive guide has delved into various facets of retail security, offering insights, practical tips, and strategies to empower businesses in safeguarding their assets, employees, and customers.

Understanding the Threat Landscape:

The guide commences by exploring the diverse threats faced by retailers. External thefts, internal thefts, casual shoplifting, organized shop robbery, and various other typologies of thefts were scrutinized. Recognizing the multifaceted nature of threats enables businesses to tailor their security measures to address specific vulnerabilities.

Legal Compliance and Operational Procedures:

A critical aspect of effective loss prevention is aligning security practices with legal frameworks. This guide emphasized the importance of adhering to the law when detaining suspects or handling theft situations. By outlining the legal procedures involved in reporting a crime and describing a suspect, retailers can mitigate risks associated with potential legal ramifications.

In instances where suspects need to be retained, the guide provided a detailed understanding of the legal procedures based on Portuguese law. Recognizing the delicate balance between detaining a suspect and avoiding unlawful confinement, businesses can navigate these situations judiciously.

Technological Solutions for Retail Security:

As technology continues to advance, integrating innovative solutions is imperative for staying ahead of potential threats. The guide delved into various technologies applicable in retail stores, from surveillance cameras and alarm systems to more sophisticated tools like facial recognition and RFID technology.

By embracing these technologies, retailers can create a layered defense against theft and unauthorized activities.

In addition to technological solutions, understanding the nuances of identifying counterfeit money and implementing measures to detect and prevent financial fraud is crucial. By staying informed about the latest advancements in security technologies, retailers can bolster their defenses against tech-savvy criminals.

Effective Communication and Training:

The guide underscored the significance of effective communication within a retail environment. Whether it's creating a common language for security incidents or establishing a code for specific situations, clear communication enhances the overall security posture of a retail establishment. Training emerged as a pivotal element in creating a security-conscious workforce.

From basic training for shopkeepers to specialized programs addressing different aspects of security, a well-informed and trained staff forms the first line of defense against potential threats.

Loss Prevention in Different Sectors:

Recognizing that various sectors within the retail industry face unique challenges, the guide provided sector-specific insights. From describing the typology of thefts in a broader social context to discussing specific actions like identifying a robber or suspect, the guide catered to the nuanced needs of different retail sectors.

Conclusion: Fostering a Culture of Security:

In conclusion, the guide advocates for the integration of security measures into the broader culture of a retail business. Creating a culture of security involves not only implementing robust technologies and procedures but also fostering a mindset that values integrity, vigilance, and continuous improvement.

Embracing a proactive approach to loss prevention positions retailers to navigate the complexities of the industry successfully.

By investing in comprehensive training programs, staying abreast of legal requirements, and leveraging cutting-edge technologies, retailers can create an environment that deters theft, ensures the safety of customers and employees, and ultimately contributes to the long-term success of the business.

As the retail landscape continues to evolve, the principles outlined in this guide provide a foundation for retailers to adapt, innovate, and fortify their security measures.

By doing so, retailers can not only protect their assets and reputation but also create a shopping environment that instills confidence and trust among consumers, ensuring sustainable growth and resilience in an ever-changing market.

ABOUT THE AUTHOR

Antonio Rosa is a seasoned security professional with a wealth of experience working in challenging and high-risk environments, particularly in Africa.

Over the years, Antonio's expertise and leadership skills enabled him to excel as a bodyguard, team leader, project manager, and ultimately, a general manager. With a specialization in Africa, he has navigated the complexities and intricacies of this diverse continent, facing, and overcoming numerous obstacles along the way.

Antonio's extensive experience in Africa has exposed him to a wide range of challenges, including dealing with high rates of criminal activities, cultural differences, religious matters, and the unique difficulties faced by expatriates. Throughout his career, Antonio has lived and worked in various countries across Africa, including Mozambique, South Africa, Namibia, and Zimbabwe.

Antonio's extensive training in Close Protection, Personal Security Detail, Marksmanship, Surveillance and Counter Surveillance and Risk Management adds valuable expertise and depth to this exceptional book. With his wealth of knowledge and experience, readers can expect to gain invaluable insights and practical advice on navigating hostile environments with confidence. Antonio's specialized skills in these areas make him a trusted authority in the field, ensuring that readers receive top-notch guidance to enhance their personal safety and security.

"In the world's most challenging environments, knowledge is your greatest ally. Keep learning, stay vigilant, and never forget: You have the power to thrive wherever your journey may lead."

www.ingramcontent.com/pod-product-compliance
Lightning Source LLC
Chambersburg PA
CBHW062325290526
45794CB00005B/1909